Overcoming
Hindrances to Receiving
the Baptism in the Holy Spirit

by
John Osteen

Lakewood Church
P.O. Box 23297
Houston, TX 77228

ISBN 0-912631-37-6

Contents

Contents

INTRODUCTION

There are literally hundreds of thousands of Christians in every denomination who hunger and thirst for the power of God. Yet, they are blocked from receiving it because they don't understand what the Bible says about the Holy Spirit.

These are good people. They are sincere people. They love Jesus. I find that most denominational Christians who are born again genuinely love the Lord. No matter what church they go to—Catholic, Baptist, Methodist, or another—they haven't received the Holy Spirit simply because they do not have light on the subject.

I was a Baptist minister for nineteen years. I served the Lord to the best of my ability. I walked in all the knowledge I had. Thank God, there came a day when He opened my understanding and gave me more light. I sought the Lord and received the baptism in the Holy Spirit. Because of the dynamic change this experience made in my ministry, as well as in my personal life, I want to help others receive the baptism in the Holy Spirit.

I graduated from college and Baptist seminary. My professors there taught me all they knew. But they knew nothing about the baptism in the Holy Spirit because they had been taught by people who didn't know anything about it. Somehow, the reality of this experience had been lost.

I was taught that the Pentecostal way was a lie. I ridiculed it. I believed, as I was taught, that the day of miracles was past and that tongues and prophecy had ceased. Praying for the sick was useless because that day was gone forever, and casting out demons was a sign of ignorance. I was convinced that a person received all that he ever would get from God when he got saved.

It took me nineteen years to wade through my seminary teaching and doctrines to receive the baptism in the Holy Spirit. I came to realize that Pentecost is not a denomination but an experience from God for everyone.

Three particular scriptures hindered me. I believe the time is here for the true interpretation of these verses to be given to the Body of Christ, because all people who know God in every denomination have a right to what God has for them.

I want to share these scriptures with you, because if you don't have the Baptism, they may be hindering you, too. And if you do have this experience, you need to know how to help others who are struggling with these obstacles.

It has been my privilege to help thousands of God's precious people from all denominations find

God's power. Now I want to help you receive it also by removing some of the hindrances that may be in your way, as they were in mine.

John Osteen

Chapter 1

You Have to Fight Pride

There is an unnatural, unified opposition to speaking in tongues in the religious realm. No other manifestation of the Spirit is so despised in the denominational world as speaking in tongues. Yet Jesus himself talked about the Holy Ghost and speaking in tongues.

In Mark 16:17, Jesus said, *These signs shall follow them that believe: In my name shall they cast out devils; they shall speak with new tongues.*

And in Acts 1:8, our Lord said, *Ye shall receive power, after that the Holy Ghost is come upon you: and ye shall be witnesses unto me both in Jerusalem, and in all Judaea, and in Samaria, and unto the uttermost part of the earth.*

Why doesn't the religious world hate miracles? Why don't they hate healings? Why don't they hate the supernatural gifts of the Spirit? Why don't they hate other manifestations of the Spirit? Why have they picked out this one single, simple demonstration of the Holy Ghost to oppose?

Because the devil knows if he can keep people from speaking in tongues, they will never receive the baptism in the Holy Spirit.

The baptism in the Holy Spirit is God's method of clothing His people with power to destroy the works of darkness. Therefore, it stands to reason that the devil would lie about it, criticize it, make fun of it, and do everything possible to hinder anyone from receiving it. Speaking in tongues is a sign to the unbeliever, the unmistakable presence and power of God Almighty. The devil wants to keep the unbeliever in the dark about God. Satan hates speaking in tongues because he knows it is also a scriptural sign to the believer that he has received the baptism in the Holy Spirit (see Acts 2,10,19, and Mark 16:17).

Actually, however, it is not speaking in tongues that hinders people and keeps them from receiving God's power. It's their pride. They say it's tongues, and the devil holds that out to them as the obstacle, but it's really not tongues. It's pride and vanity.

A humbling experience

Isaiah 28:11,12 says, *For with stammering lips and another tongue will he speak to this people. To whom he said, This is the rest wherewith ye may cause the weary to rest; and this is the refreshing.*

The Amplified Version of this verse speaks of the stammering lips and another tongue as "a more humiliating way."

So many people in our world who belong to Jesus still need that rest and refreshing and power of God in their lives. Yet, they are held back from receiving it because, in a sense, it is a humiliating experience. God's Spirit humbles you, because to receive the Baptism you must empty yourself of pride.

I know because my Baptist pride was as high as the heavens. I had my degrees. I had a successful ministry. Why, it was humiliating to think that I would be asked to identify with people who talked in other tongues.

Do you see the problem? You must overcome your pride to be filled with the Holy Spirit.

A distinguished company

The people who speak in other tongues are a good crowd to be in, but I didn't know that. Paul the apostle, Peter, James, John, and the Blessed Virgin Mary, the mother of Jesus, all spoke in tongues. What an honor to be in their company!

I was in Mexico a few years ago with a group of men and the driver assigned to our car was a university student. We were talking about the baptism in the Holy Spirit, but we couldn't get this student interested.

One of the men in our party was sitting in the front seat, talking to this driver in Spanish. I was sitting in the back seat. Hearing them converse in Spanish set me off to speaking in tongues. When I hear somebody talk in another language, I like to talk my language. So, sitting in the back seat, I just put up my hands and began to worship the Lord in other tongues.

With this, the young man pulled over and stopped. "What kind of language are you speaking?" he asked.

11

Knowing he was a devout Catholic, I said, "Oh, I'm talking the same language the Blessed Virgin talked on the Day of Pentecost."

From that moment on, the young student was with us everywhere we went. We couldn't get rid of him. He wanted to talk the language the Blessed Virgin talked.

One of the greatest barriers to receiving the baptism in the Holy Spirit is an unwillingness to humble ourselves. If tongues has been a barrier to you, search the scriptures with an open mind. Don't study to disprove tongues, simply read and meditate upon God's Word as you seek for His light upon the subject. A teachable spirit will lead you into the fullness of God's power and Spirit.

Chapter 2

Hindrance Number One:
You automatically receive the
Holy Ghost when you get saved

As a Baptist minister, I longed for the power of God. I craved it. I knew I did not have all God wanted me to have. But as I read the Bible, certain scriptures about the Holy Spirit disturbed me. I had the wrong interpretation of them; therefore, they were hindrances to me.

The first scripture was Romans 8:9, which says, *But ye are not in the flesh, but in the Spirit, if so be that the Spirit of God dwell in you. Now if any man have not the Spirit of Christ, he is none of his.*

Pentecostal people, seeing my desire for God's power, would come up to me and say, "Brother Osteen, you need the Holy Ghost."

Well, I knew I had the Holy Ghost. Every Christian is born of the Spirit. Jesus said, *Except a man be born of water and of the Spirit, he cannot enter into the kingdom of God* (John 3:5).

You are born again by the Spirit of God. The Holy Ghost does a work in you at salvation. He performs a divine miracle in your heart called the new

13

birth. Then He witnesses with your spirit and tells you that you are a child of God. Romans 8:16 says, *The Spirit itself beareth witness with our spirit, that we are the children of God.*

Every Christian is regenerated by the Holy Spirit. But this is not the baptism in the Holy Spirit.

Jesus, who is the Head of the Church, said, *I will pray the Father, and he shall give you another Comforter* [now, who would refuse to take a comforter?], *that he may abide with you for ever; Even the Spirit of truth; WHOM THE WORLD CANNOT RECEIVE, because it seeth him not, neither knoweth him: but ye know him; for he dwelleth with you, and shall be in you* (John 14:16,17, emphasis mine).

Did you know that when you came to Jesus to receive this new birth, you were *in* the world and *of* the world? Paul said, ...*in times past ye walked according to the course of this world...and were by nature the children of wrath* (Ephesians 2:2,3). So at the time you came to accept Jesus as your Savior, you were not ready to receive the Holy Ghost. You came to receive forgiveness. You came to receive eternal life and to become a child of God. Only then were you ready to receive the Holy Ghost.

The Holy Spirit is for Christians, not sinners

Before I was saved, I was of the world. And the world, according to Jesus, cannot receive the Holy Ghost. Salvation is for sinners. The baptism in the Holy Spirit is for Christians. Let me illustrate this truth from the Word of God.

On one of the Apostle Paul's journeys, he came to Ephesus and there met some disciples. He said to them, *Have ye received the Holy Ghost since ye believed?* (Acts 19:2).

If we automatically receive the Holy Ghost when we believe on Christ, this would have been a foolish question, wouldn't it? Why would Paul ask this question if everyone received the Holy Ghost when they got saved?

And they said unto him, We have not so much as heard whether there be any Holy Ghost.

And he said unto them, Unto what then were ye baptized? And they said, Unto John's baptism.

Then said Paul, John verily baptized with the baptism of repentance, saying unto the people, that they should believe on him which should come after him, that is, on Christ Jesus.

When they heard this, they were baptized in the name of the Lord Jesus. And when Paul had laid his hands upon them, the Holy Ghost came on them; and they spake with tongues, and prophesied (Acts 19:2-6).

Now scriptures like this kept me from the Baptism for nineteen long years. I want to break down every barrier, tear away every curtain so that every child of God in every denomination can be Spirit-filled and have the glory of God in their lives.

To see that the new birth is not the same as the baptism in the Holy Spirit, read Acts, chapter 8. These verses are an account of one of the greatest revivals of the Early Church, which was conducted by Philip in the city of Samaria. They clearly show that new Christians received this experience AFTER they were saved.

Supernatural things happened when Philip preached under the anointing of the Holy Ghost. Verse 7 says, *Unclean spirits, crying with loud voice, came out of many that were possessed with them: and many taken with palsies, and that were lame, were healed.*

Because of these miracles, there was great joy among the people. Verse 12 says, *When they believed Philip preaching the things concerning the kingdom of God, and the name of Jesus Christ, they were baptized, both men and women.*

Do you believe Philip would baptize unsaved people? No way. Certainly these people were saved. They became believers. When they believed what Philip was preaching about Jesus, they were born again, and Philip baptized them in water. They were water-baptized believers, but not yet filled with the Holy Ghost.

Verse 14 says, *Now when the apostles which were at Jerusalem heard that Samaria had received the word of God, they sent unto them Peter and John.*

I'm going to quote verse 15 *incorrectly*, because many churches act as if it reads this way:

"Who, when they were come down, said unto them, You got it all when you got saved. Don't worry about getting anything else. And don't let anybody talk to you about speaking in tongues or getting any baptism in the Holy Spirit."

Is that what it says? No!

Now let's read it correctly. It says, *Who, when they were come down, prayed for them, that they might receive the Holy Ghost.*

16

For as yet he was fallen upon none of them: only they were baptized [in water] *in the name of the Lord Jesus* (vs. 16).

The baptism in the Holy Spirit is the experience Jesus was talking about in John 14. You can readily see from these verses that it is totally different from salvation.

Chapter 3

Hindrance Number Two: The same Spirit that saves you, baptizes you in the Holy Spirit

The second scripture that bothered me is found in 1 Corinthians 12:12,13. This text, especially, troubled me. I would long for more power, and I'd come to the point of being almost ready to believe in the baptism in the Holy Spirit. Then I'd read these verses, and my interpretation of them from college and seminary just blasted me out, and I would give up again. This happened many times.

It says, *For as the body is one, and hath many members, and all the members of that one body, being many, are one body: so also is Christ.*

For by one Spirit are we all baptized into one body, whether we be Jews or Gentiles, whether we be bond or free; and have been all made to drink into one Spirit.

When I would read those verses, I'd say, "Well, evidently I got the baptism in the Holy Spirit when I got saved. This scripture says we are all baptized by one Spirit into the Body of Christ. So I guess I'll just have to wait until I get to Heaven to get what I'm longing for."

Have you ever thought that?

These verses are not talking about the baptism in the Holy Spirit. They are talking about the work of the Spirit when you get saved and receive the new birth. This is when the Holy Ghost baptizes, or immerses you into the Body of Christ, the Church.

You don't have to join the true Church. You're born into it. I don't mean when you're born as a baby; I mean when you are born again. When a sinner accepts Jesus as Savior, he is not only born again, but he is baptized, placed into the Body of Christ and thus automatically becomes a member of the one true Church. *For by one Spirit are we all baptized into one body*. At that moment, the Holy Ghost regenerates you and makes you a new creature.

Therefore if any man be in Christ, he is a new creature: old things are passed away; behold, all things are become new (2 Corinthians 5:17).

Jesus referred to the experience of receiving the Holy Ghost as a "baptism." In Acts 1:4,5, He commanded His disciples not to depart from Jerusalem, but to wait there for the promise of the Father, which He had told them about. He said, *For John truly baptized with water; but ye shall be BAPTIZED with the Holy Ghost not many days hence* (emphasis mine).

Keep the word "baptism" uppermost in your mind, and you will understand what Jesus meant here.

The meaning of baptism

Baptism, which is *baptismo* in the Greek, means "to dip under." And in any baptism by immersion there must be three things.

• First of all, there must be a baptizer.

• Secondly, there must be a candidate to be baptized.

• Thirdly, there must be an element in which to baptize or immerse the candidate.

In water baptism, the minister who does the baptizing is the baptizer, the element is water, and the born-again believer is the candidate. You can't have a baptism without those three things.

Now let's look for these three things in the Baptism 1 Corinthians 12:13 is talking about. They are clearly set forth.

For by one Spirit are we all baptized into one body.

Who is the Baptizer here? The Holy Spirit.

What is the element? The Body of Christ. In water baptism, we are baptized into the Body of Christ, the true Church.

Then who is the candidate? The saved person, the believer who has accepted Jesus as Lord and Savior.

This is regeneration—the new birth. When we speak of the baptism in the Holy Spirit, however, we are not talking about something the Holy Ghost does to you, but something Jesus does to you. Jesus is the Baptizer in the Holy Spirit.

In Matthew 3:11, John the Baptist said, *I indeed baptize you with water unto repentance: but he that cometh after me is mightier than I* [who is John talking about? Jesus!], *whose shoes I am not worthy to bear* [untie or unloose]: *he shall baptize you with the Holy Ghost, and with fire*.

So Jesus is the Baptizer in the baptism in the Holy Spirit. The saved person who belongs to God, who is washed in the blood of Jesus and made the righteousness of God, is the candidate. And the Holy Ghost is the One the candidate is baptized into.

When this happens, the scripture comes to pass which says, *Ye shall receive power, after that the Holy Ghost is come upon you* (Acts 1:8).

I believe that now you can see the difference between being baptized by the HOLY SPIRIT *into* the Body of Christ and then being baptized by JESUS *in* the Holy Spirit.

Chapter 4

Hindrance Number Three: You don't have to speak in tongues to be baptized in the Holy Spirit

When I finally hurdled the first two scriptures that hindered me from receiving God's Spirit, I had a head-on confrontation with one more hindrance in a third scripture.

People often get to a certain point of believing in the Baptism, then make one last attempt at holding out. They use the old argument, "Yes, the baptism in the Holy Spirit is real. Yes, some people speak in tongues. But not everyone who receives the Baptism speaks in tongues, and I want to be one of those who doesn't."

That is exactly the way I thought because of my understanding of 1 Corinthians 12:28-31:

And God hath set some in the church, first apostles, secondarily prophets, thirdly teachers, after that miracles, then gifts of healings, helps, governments, diversities of tongues.

Are all apostles? [The answer is no.] *are all prophets?* [The answer is no again.] *are all teachers?* [The answer is still no.] *are all workers of miracles?*

[Of course not.] *Have all the gifts of healing*? [No, they don't.] *DO ALL SPEAK WITH TONGUES*? [The answer is no.] *do all interpret*? [The answer is no again.]

But covet earnestly the best gifts: and yet shew I unto you a more excellent way (emphasis mine).

Now I have to be honest. I don't care whether it upsets my doctrine or not, I'm going to stay with the Bible no matter who it separates me from or who it identifies me with. I did violence to the scriptures for nineteen years, and I will not do it anymore. The answer to these questions is no. And I can almost hear someone saying, "Oh, thank God, I knew I didn't have to speak in tongues to be baptized in the Holy Spirit. I'm going to get it a dignified way."

There is no dignified way to be filled with the Holy Ghost. You can forget that way of thinking.

A fellow once wrote to me, "Brother Osteen, I don't mind getting the Baptism if I don't have to clap my hands and lift my arms, or speak in tongues and pray for the sick and cast out devils."

"Well," I wrote him back, "you don't even need it!"

I'll never forget a denominational preacher who came up to me when I first got the Baptism. He was angry. He called me by my full name. "John Osteen…" When someone knows me by my first name but they call me by my full name, I know they are serious. And that's what he did.

He said, "John Osteen, I want you to know this. I don't need the baptism in the Holy Spirit or the power that you're talking about for what I'm doing."

I said, "Brother, I agree. In your church, you don't cast out devils. You don't lay hands on the sick. You don't believe in miracles. You don't believe in the supernatural. You're right. You don't need the Holy Ghost for what you're doing. You're playing church.

"But my brother," I said, "listen to me. The divine, supreme Head of the Church—the Lord Jesus Christ, the King of kings and Lord of lords, the King of the universe, the One who has all power in Heaven and earth, the Lily of the Valley, the Bright and Morning Star, He who stood in Revelation and said, *I am he that liveth, and was dead; and, behold, I am alive for evermore*—this Jesus, who walks among the churches and watches their affairs and who holds the ministers in His right hand, said, 'I command you to do the works that I do. Cast out devils, raise the dead, lay hands on the sick, and do the works that are supernatural.'"

I said, "Brother, when you realize that you've got that kind of work to do, and you become aware of your total lack of power to do that work, you'll be on your knees begging for the baptism in the Holy Spirit."

For years the question, *Do all speak with tongues?* kept me from receiving the Baptism. I said, "Well, it might really be a genuine experience, and some might speak in tongues, but surely not all, because the answer to Paul's scriptural question is no."

Two kinds of speaking in tongues

I did not realize then that there are two kinds of speaking in tongues. The first is in connection with the gifts of the Spirit. There are nine supernatural gifts of the Spirit, and one of these gifts is *divers kinds of tongues* (1 Corinthians 12:10).

But there is also another manifestation of the Holy Ghost whereby we speak in tongues, which we call "glossalalia" or "the prayer language." The prayer language is a release of your spirit to bypass your mind and talk to God spirit-to-Spirit.

First Corinthians 14:2 refers to this kind of speaking in tongues. It says, *He that speaketh in an unknown tongue speaketh not unto men, but unto God: for no man understandeth him; howbeit in the spirit he speaketh mysteries.*

This is different from the gift of tongues.

In the gift of tongues, you speak unto men, not unto God. Concerning the operation of the gift of tongues, the Bible says, *Let all things be done unto edifying. If any man speak in an unknown tongue, let it be by two, or at the most by three, and that by course; and let one interpret* (1 Corinthians 14:26,27).

For instance, if I were to give a message in tongues in church, I would speak out to the congregation and someone there would, in the Spirit, understand what I was saying. They would then give the interpretation of what I said by the gift of tongues so the Church could be enlightened, instructed, and built up spiritually. This is called the gift of tongues and the gift of interpretation of tongues.

When you exercise the gift of tongues, what you are saying in tongues is directed to the people. Then there is an interpretation. Somebody will understand in the Spirit what you have spoken in tongues and give an interpretation for the purpose of edifying the Church.

The prayer language you get when you are baptized in the Holy Spirit is not spoken out to people, but upward to God. It is a language that comes up out of your spirit in prayer and worship to God. The Bible says, *God is a Spirit: and they that worship him must worship him in spirit and in truth* (John 4:24).

You see, there is a spirit man living on the inside of your body. Your spirit man is real. He has eyes. Ephesians 1:18 speaks of *the eyes of your understanding being enlightened.* Your spirit man has ears. You can hear what the world cannot hear. Your spirit man has a voice and a mouth. When I communicate with people, I use my mind and my vocal cords to express myself. When I talk in tongues and pray to the Father, I use my vocal cords, but my spirit man bypasses my mind and talks to God spirit-to-Spirit with my prayer language.

Romans 8:26,27 refers to this phenomenon. *Likewise the Spirit also helpeth our infirmities: for we know not what we should pray for as we ought: but the Spirit itself maketh intercession for us with groanings which cannot be uttered. And he* [God] *that searcheth the hearts knoweth what is the mind of the Spirit* [understands what the Spirit is saying] *because he maketh intercession for the saints according to the will of God.*

When you receive the baptism in the Holy Spirit, you receive a prayer language, whereby your spirit is released to talk to the Father about whatever is troubling you. We don't always know what to pray for, or how to pray as we should. But the Spirit himself helps us and prays for our needs in harmony with God's will. Can you think of anything more tremendous than this?

"Well," you may say, "on the Day of Pentecost the people understood what the disciples were saying in other tongues when they received the Holy Ghost. That must have been the gift of tongues."

What happened on the Day of Pentecost

Let me explain what I believe happened on the Day of Pentecost. The Bible tells us that there were many godly people in Jerusalem for the religious celebrations taking place at that time. When they heard the noise of the outpouring of the Holy Spirit, a great crowd gathered to see what the commotion was all about.

The disciples all received the prayer language when they were filled with the Holy Ghost that day. The language the people heard the disciples speaking was the prayer language of the Spirit. It sounded like a bunch of garbled talk to the Jews, and they said, *These men are full of new wine* (Acts 2:13).

"They are drunk!" they said. The disciples were drunk, but not on wine. They were intoxicated on the new wine of the Holy Spirit.

I believe that then God immediately manifested the gift of tongues, and the people who had gathered began to understand in their own languages what the disciples were saying in tongues.

Acts 2:7,8,11 says, *And they were all amazed and marvelled, saying one to another, Behold, are not all these which speak Galilaeans? And how hear we every man in our own tongue, wherein we were born?*

28

We do hear them speak in our tongues the wonderful works of God.

The prayer language is for your private use. Of course, a church can pray and worship together in the prayer language by common consent. But these tongues are essentially for your private use.

The Apostle Paul spoke in tongues. He said, *I thank my God, I speak with tongues more than ye all: Yet in the church I had rather speak five words with my understanding, that by my voice I might teach others also, than ten thousand words in an unknown tongue* (1 Corinthians 14:18,19).

If I got up in the pulpit on Sunday morning and spoke in the prayer language for an hour, you might as well stay home and sleep late. You wouldn't understand anything I was saying. Paul said that it is far better to speak five words in a language a church congregation can understand than ten thousand in tongues.

When I received the baptism in the Holy Spirit, I spoke in other tongues, and have continued to do so daily since that wonderful time.

Far be it from me to downplay or censure speaking in tongues. With the Apostle Paul, I say, *I would that ye all spake with tongues*, and, *Forbid not to speak with tongues* (1 Corinthians 14:5,39). My desire, like Paul, is to *speak with tongues more than ye all* (vs. 18).

What a tremendous blessing it is for the Spirit of God to move upon us, enabling us to pray in other languages or give a message in tongues for the edification of the Church!

Chapter 5

The Purpose of This Experience

One of the questions people ask most often concerning the baptism in the Holy Spirit is, "What is the purpose of this experience?"

God baptizes you in the Holy Spirit, not just so you can speak in tongues but that you might have power. The whole purpose of this experience is to give you power.

In 1958, as a Southern Baptist minister, I was burdened to win the lost and bring deliverance to suffering humanity. But to do that, I needed power that I didn't possess.

Hungering for more of God, I set my heart to seek the Lord. I began fasting and reading the Word. As I studied the Bible, the glorious Son of God, who was above and beyond anything I had ever dreamed, emerged from its pages. He wanted to be in our day. There He stood, bigger than all our sufferings and problems, having never lost one bit of His power or compassion.

I saw that humanity was blinded by the devil and held in the grip of his satanic power. I saw Satan going forth as a roaring lion to kill, steal, and destroy.

In contrast, I saw that Jesus came as the Mighty Conqueror to destroy the works of the devil. He said, *All POWER is given unto me in heaven and in earth* and, *Ye shall receive POWER, after that the Holy Ghost is come upon you* (Matthew 28:18, Acts 1:8, emphasis mine).

I learned that Jesus never performed a single miracle, nor even began His earthly ministry, until He had been baptized in the Holy Spirit. He said that He did nothing outside the power of the Holy Ghost. The Holy Spirit filled Jesus, giving Him His power.

The same power Jesus had

As I prayed before the Lord, He baptized me in the Holy Spirit and fire. I had the same power that Peter, Paul, and all the early disciples had. I received the same power that Jesus spoke of when He said, *The Spirit of the Lord is upon me, because he hath anointed me to preach the gospel to the poor; he hath sent me to heal the brokenhearted, to preach deliverance to the captives, and recovering of sight to the blind, to set at liberty them that are bruised, to preach the acceptable year of the Lord* (Luke 4:18,19).

The same power that helped Jesus do His work was now in me. My life and ministry has not been the same since. From that time, I went forth with the Full Gospel message and with the power of God. People were saved, healed, and delivered. New churches were started. New converts were left with joy and power. Devils came out of people, and captives were set free.

The baptism in the Holy Spirit is the doorway to God's supernatural power. Jesus said, *He that believeth on me, the works that I do shall he do also; and greater works than these shall he do; because I go unto my Father* (John 14:12).

Again Jesus said, *These signs shall follow them that believe; In my name shall they cast out devils; they shall speak with new tongues; They shall take up serpents; and if they drink any deadly thing, it shall not hurt them; they shall lay hands on the sick, and they shall recover* (Mark 16:17,18).

The baptism in the Holy Spirit is to enable you to fulfill these scriptures. When the disciples received the baptism in the Holy Spirit, they received power to do the same works that Jesus did. And so will you.

God does not give us His precious Holy Spirit to enjoy alone and forget the needs of the world. It is not His purpose for us to get together just to shout, talk in tongues, prophesy over one another, and feast upon some "new revelation" while the world rushes on toward hell.

The purpose of the Holy Ghost is to empower the Church to take the Gospel of Jesus Christ to this needy world. Joel 3:13,14 says, *Put ye in the sickle, for the harvest is ripe: come, get you down; for the press is full, the vats overflow; for their wickedness is great. Multitudes, multitudes in the valley of decision: for the day of the Lord is near in the valley of decision.*

The Prophet Joel said the harvest is ripe now. The desperate need of our generation is far too serious to play games. The hands of a sighing, crying, dying world are outstretched and their hearts are open. People will believe and receive Jesus when they see the same power and miracles that He performed on earth being performed in lives today. This is what happens when you receive the baptism in the Holy Spirit.

Chapter 6

The Baptism in the Holy Spirit Is for Everyone

Thank God, this experience is for everyone who longs for more of God. The Word says that on the last day of the great feast, *Jesus stood and cried, saying, If any man thirst, let him come unto me, and drink. He that believeth on me, as the scripture hath said, out of his belly shall flow rivers of living water.*

(But this spake he of the Spirit, which they that believe on him should receive: for the Holy Ghost was not yet given; because that Jesus was not yet glorified) (John 7:37-39).

If any man thirst...any person—man, woman, boy, or girl, anybody, anywhere—who has a desire and a longing for the supernatural power of God, can have it. You don't have to turn to witchcraft and astrology. You don't have to turn to Satan worship. You don't have to turn to eastern religions, or anything like that. You can have the real thing.

It doesn't matter whether you're Catholic, Presbyterian, Lutheran, or what church you belong to or attend. God does not look for denominational labels.

If there is a longing in your heart to know God better, Jesus is talking about you.

I want to point out to you what this scripture does NOT say. It does not say, "If any man thirst, let him go to the nearest Pentecostal church, because that is the only place you can get help." I thank God for Pentecostal people and for everyone who is filled with the Spirit. But no one owns this experience. Jesus is the Baptizer in the Holy Spirit.

When I was a Baptist, I was scared of Pentecostals. They made me nervous. I felt out of place around them. I wasn't used to being around people who said, "Praise Goooooddd! Halleluuuuuujah!" They didn't say, "Hallelujah" at all like I was used to hearing it!

I remember when I first began getting interested in the baptism in the Holy Spirit, I rode around in a car with a Pentecostal preacher one day to talk and fellowship with him. I wanted to find out more about the Baptism. He shouted hallelujah and glory to God so much I just scooted down in the car and hid. It was embarrassing. I didn't want anybody to see me riding with him.

I didn't know then what I've learned about praising and worshiping God. God enjoys the praises of His people. The psalmist said, *Let every thing that hath breath praise the Lord* (Psalm 150:6). David said, *I will bless the Lord at all times: his praise shall continually be in my mouth...the humble shall hear thereof, and be glad* (Psalm 34:1,2).

Notice, that verse says it's the humble who will be glad, not the proud. If you are full of pride, you won't be glad. If you are thirsty for God, rejoice. God gave you that thirst. There are thirsty people all over this world. And Jesus said, *If any man thirst, let him come unto me, and drink.*

A preacher who thirsted

One day I got a call from a minister on the East Coast. He is an example of how God draws people to Him and makes them thirsty. When I picked up the phone, the voice on the other end of the line said, "Pastor Osteen, I'm a Baptist preacher. I understand that you have received the baptism in the Holy Spirit."

I replied, "Yes, I have."

"I'm interested in this experience," he said, "but I'm wondering about speaking in tongues."

I said, "Brother, don't waste your time on a long distance call. When you receive the baptism in the Holy Spirit, you're going to speak in tongues. You're calling me to see if I can talk you out of that, but I'm not going to. You'll speak in tongues if you ever get the Baptism."

He said, "Thank you," and hung up.

In a few days this preacher called back and said, "Brother Osteen, I'm the man that hung up on you a few days ago. But I'm thirsty. I want the baptism in the Holy Spirit."

I said, "If you are thirsty and you seek God with an open heart, you're going to receive. And when you do, you're going to speak in tongues. There is no way to keep your dignity and your denominational pride. When you get the Holy Ghost, you're going to speak in tongues just like all the rest of us. Not only that, there are some people who are going to hate you and despise you because of it."

37

He said, "Thank you," and hung up again. But in a few days, this minister called back a third time. He and his wife were visiting relatives.

He said, "Brother Osteen, my wife wants me to visit with her relatives, but I can't visit. I'm so thirsty for God I can't visit, read the newspaper, watch TV, listen to the radio, or anything else. I left my wife at her folks' house and got in the car and drove out in the country and just sat there.

"While I was sitting in the car, I felt two hands laid on my hands, and I heard a voice in my spirit saying, 'Go to Houston and let John Osteen lay his hands on you and you'll receive the Holy Ghost.'"

I said, "Brother, I don't receive that. Don't make something big out of me. You don't have to have me to get the Holy Ghost. You can receive the Baptism right there. God is where you are as well as here."

I paused, and he said, "Yes, but you didn't hear the voice. The church here took up an offering to buy my plane fare to come to Houston."

What could I say? You see, Jesus touches people and makes them thirsty.

Can't you just see this man getting on that plane and flying all the way from the East Coast, weeping, yearning for God? Oh, this kind of spirit touches God! Some people wouldn't walk down a church aisle to receive the blessed baptism in the Holy Spirit from the hands of Jesus himself. Yet there are people who will cross a nation, who will go around the world, to receive the Holy Ghost.

I took two men from our church with me to the airport to meet this minister. We had never seen him,

38

and I wondered how we would recognize him. But it isn't hard to recognize the long, lean, hungry look of a person thirsting after God.

When this preacher got off the plane, tears were rolling down his face, and we recognized him right away. As we put him in the car and started driving from the airport, I noticed his hands were shaking. God's Spirit was all over him. I thought, *We'd better leave him alone in this car. He's going to have to have plenty of room when Jesus baptizes him.*

Curtis Bell, one of the men with me, had built a little place in his home especially for people who wanted to get the Baptism. He would keep them in his house and pray with them. So we took this minister there.

As soon as he set his suitcases down, I said, "Let's first just pray a little while." I asked the preacher to kneel in the middle of the room. Then we all found places to pray so that we surrounded him in prayer.

As we were praying, the Lord spoke to me and said, "Didn't he say if he would come to Houston and you'd lay your hands on him that I'd baptize him in the Holy Spirit?"

I said, "Yes, God, that's what he said."

"Then why are you sitting over here in this corner praying?" God asked. "Go over there and put your hands on him!"

So I slipped up behind the minister and put my hands on him as he was praying. The very moment my hands touched him, he stopped speaking English. He rose up and lifted his hands in worship and surrender to God, and the language of the Holy Ghost

39

began to pour out of him. He talked in tongues and talked in tongues. Then he talked in tongues some more. He worshiped God and talked in tongues for what seemed like hours.

He walked up to Brother Bell and tried to tell him how wonderful the Holy Ghost was, but couldn't speak any English. He could only speak in tongues. He tried to tell me how wonderful it was, and he only spoke in tongues more.

It was getting late, and we all needed to go to bed to get our rest. Finally, I took him by the arm and led him to his bedroom. I laid him down, took off his shoes and socks and pulled the covers over him. When I left him, he was still speaking in tongues.

The next day, he said, "Brother Osteen, if you thought it was good when you put me to bed, you should have been here when I woke up!"

There was no doubt about it. The Lord had baptized this man in the Holy Spirit. Rivers of living water were flowing out of his innermost being.

Not everyone receives the baptism in the Holy Spirit in this manner. Some receive it joyfully, but quietly. However, I've never known anyone to receive it without speaking in tongues.

Other thirsty souls

I used to pray for anybody, anywhere to receive the baptism in the Holy Spirit whether they wanted it or not. I wanted everyone to receive it. I'd run around them and shout like a Commanche Indian, and they would sit like wooden Indians. But I quit that.

Jesus said, "If any man thirst, let him come to Me and drink. I'll quench his thirst. I'll fill him to overflowing with My Spirit!" I soon learned that if a person is not interested, you're better off to forget it. Save your time and energy for those who really want it. You'll never have enough time to get around to all the thirsty ones. There are people all over the world who desire the Holy Ghost. Our business is to help them.

I remember an ex-governor who called me and said, "Brother Osteen, I want the baptism in the Holy Spirit. I'm coming to Houston to get it."

He arrived in Houston on a bus, and I met him. I'd never had a governor or an ex-governor in my home, and I didn't know what to do with him. He walked into my home and I said, "I'll tell you what, Governor. I'll put you in a motel. You read the Bible and pray and we'll talk to you tomorrow."

Now governors are men of decision. I'll never forget what he said. He stood up—all six foot six—and looked down at me and said, "I didn't come here to go to a motel. I came here to get the Holy Ghost." And he got it!

I'll never forget another man, the owner of a trucking company in Illinois. He was chairman of the deacons in his church. Yet, he was on the brink of suicide because of troubles and sorrow and a lack of power in his life. That hungry-hearted man rode a bus down to Houston and got the baptism in the Holy Spirit and fire. As far as I know, he is still going strong for God.

Now, Houston is a good place. But a person doesn't have to come to Houston, Texas, to receive the baptism in the Holy Spirit. If you came, we would pray with you. But Jesus said that you must come to HIM and drink.

Did you know there is something that nobody can do for you? No one can swallow for you. Swallowing is a very personal thing. You can swallow all day long and it won't affect me. Jesus said, "If anyone thirst, let him come to Me and drink. I'm the Baptizer." Every person has to exercise faith and drink for himself.

"Then," Jesus said, "out of his belly, or innermost being will flow rivers of living water."

When you get saved, you get satisfied. You have the joy of knowing you are going to Heaven. When you receive the baptism in the Holy Spirit, you get RIVERS of living water which flow out to a needy world with signs and wonders and miracles.

I have good news. If you want the Holy Spirit, thank God, you can have it. *For the promise is unto you, and to your children, and to all that are afar off, even as many as the Lord our God shall call* (Acts 2:39). God's power to help suffering humanity and to live an overcoming Christian life is for everyone who desires it and seeks it.

Chapter 7

How You Can Be Baptized in the Holy Spirit

I pray that in the preceding chapters I have helped you work through some of the hindrances that may have kept you from receiving the baptism in the Holy Spirit. Now I want to share with you how you can receive this wonderful experience.

Some people have made a religious doctrine out of how one should receive the baptism in the Holy Spirit. Usually, they have their formulas for how it works, but very little Bible knowledge on the subject.

It's important for you to know that everybody does not receive the Baptism in the same way. God was careful to give us examples in His Word about how it is received so that we would not invent some kind of formula or rigid idea that you have to follow to get it. But don't let anyone tell you otherwise. When you receive the Holy Spirit, you will speak in tongues. This is the scriptural evidence that you have been baptized in God's Holy Spirit.

The Scriptures show us many varied ways to receive the Holy Spirit. For instance, Peter preaching on the Day of Pentecost said, *Repent, and be baptized every one of you in the name of Jesus Christ for the remission of sins, and ye shall receive the gift of the Holy Ghost* (Acts 2:38).

Some people have understood this scripture to say the *only* way to receive the baptism in the Holy Spirit is by repenting and being baptized in the Name of Jesus Christ. But this presents only *one* way to receive God's power. The Apostle Paul received the Baptism through the laying on of hands by Ananias, an ordinary layman. Acts 9:17,18 says, *And Ananias went his way, and entered into the house; and putting his hands on him said, Brother Saul, the Lord, even Jesus, that appeared unto thee in the way as thou camest, hath sent me, that thou mightest receive thy sight, and be filled with the Holy Ghost.*

And immediately there fell from his eyes as it had been scales: and he received sight forthwith, and arose, and was baptized.

Some people might conclude from those verses that you must have hands laid on you to receive the Baptism. However, in Acts 10:44-46 we read where Cornelius and his entire household received the Baptism as Peter preached to them.

While Peter yet spake these words, the Holy Ghost fell on all them which heard the word. And they of the circumcision which believed were astonished, as many as came with Peter, because that on the Gentiles also was poured out the gift of the Holy Ghost. For they heard them speak with tongues, and magnify God.

Cornelius' household did not get baptized in water first, nor were hands laid upon them. The Holy Spirit fell on them as they heard the Word.

In another instance, recorded in Acts 19:2-6, the Christians at Ephesus received the Holy Spirit who had never even heard of the Baptism.

[Paul] *said unto them, Have ye received the Holy Ghost since ye believed? And they said unto him, We have not so much as heard whether there be any Holy Ghost.*

And he said unto them, Unto what then were ye baptized? And they said, Unto John's baptism. Then said Paul, John verily baptized with the baptism of repentance, saying unto the people, that they should believe on him which should come after him, that is, on Christ Jesus.

When they heard this, they were baptized in the name of the Lord Jesus. And when Paul had laid his hands upon them, the Holy Ghost came on them; and they spake with tongues, and prophesied.

These Christians had never heard of the baptism in the Holy Spirit, but they were teachable. As soon as Paul told them about the Baptism, they believed and received.

God is a God of variety. Do not try to limit Him. Jesus is the Baptizer, and He will baptize you the way He wants to if you are truly thirsting for this experience.

Know you are born again

To receive the baptism in the Holy Spirit, you must first know that you have been born again. A lot of people try to receive God's power who do not truly know what it means to be born again. Many "religious" people have never repented of their sins and truly accepted Jesus as their Savior. They have never turned from their old life.

When I received the Holy Spirit, I was working in the insurance business and pastoring occasionally. In the business world, I met men who would curse in one breath and talk about Jesus in another.

I remember one day I went into a man's office. As we talked, he began to curse and swear. I said, "Did you ever think about becoming a Christian?" He pointed to a big book on his desk and said, "That's the book for the deeper spiritual life class in our church, and I'm the teacher!"

Dear God! I thought. It was enough to make the angels weep. When a person is genuinely born again, he turns away from cursing, drinking, lying, cheating, stealing, adultery, wickedness, uncleanness, and all the works of the world, the flesh, and the devil.

If you do not have the assurance of salvation, you CAN have it. Romans 10:9,10 says, *If thou shalt confess with thy mouth the Lord Jesus, and shalt believe in thine heart that God hath raised him from the dead, thou shalt be saved. For with the heart man believeth unto righteousness; and with the mouth confession is made unto salvation.*

God wants to save you. Pray this prayer with me, and you can be born again:

"Dear God, I do not want to be lost. I want to be saved. Lord Jesus, come into my heart right now and save me. Wash me in Your blood and cleanse me from my sins. From this moment, I turn from my old ways and my old life. I make You the Lord of my life. Thank You for saving me and for helping me to live the rest of my life for You. Amen."

Accept the Spirit as God's gift

The Holy Spirit is a gift from God just as salvation is a gift. God's gift to the sinner is eternal life. His gift to the Christian is the Holy Spirit.

Jesus said, *If a son shall ask bread of any of you that is a father, will he give him a stone? or if he ask a fish, will he for a fish give him a serpent? Of if he shall ask an egg, will he offer him a scorpion? If ye then, being evil, know how to give good gifts unto your children: how much more shall your heavenly Father GIVE the Holy Spirit to them that ask him?* (Luke 11:11-13, emphasis mine).

You do not have to do penance or bribe God for this gift. Neither can you earn it by your holiness or goodness. Do not worry about trying to give up this or that before you receive. Get the full glory of the Spirit inside you. Then you will have power to break any habit or overcome any hindrance to a holy life. Acts 1:8 says that you will receive power AFTER the Holy Ghost comes upon you.

Base your experience on God's Word

Study the Word. Know what it says. Then believe God will do what He says in His Word. Hebrews 11:6 says, *Without faith it is impossible to please* [God]; *for he that cometh to God must believe that he is, and that he is a rewarder of them that diligently seek him.*

Do not cling to some denominational name tag and say, "My church does not believe in the baptism in the Holy Ghost." God never started any denomination. He loves every person in every denomination, and His power is for every child of God. It is not important what Catholics believe, or Methodists, or Presbyterians. What is important is what the Word of God says.

If you hold tightly to your church doctrines and never read your Bible, you will be blind to the truth of God. But if you study God's Word with an open mind, and believe that what God promises He will fulfill, you will receive the baptism in the Holy Spirit.

Praise God

A Baptist lady who received the Holy Spirit in one of our revivals said, "All they had to do was teach me how to praise the Lord. When I learned to do that, it was easy to receive the Holy Spirit."

How true this is. Most Christians do not know how to truly worship and praise the Lord. When you praise God, your spirit is reaching out and up to God. Praise is adoration. It is worship.

Let yourself go and begin to praise the Name of the Lord. Lift your hands up high in the air as a sign of complete surrender and rejoice in Him. Begin to praise and thank Jesus for the promise of the Holy Spirit and because He has washed away your sins by His blood. People do not get filled with the Spirit by crying and begging God for it. They receive as they praise and worship the Lord and magnify Him.

The power of the Spirit comes from *within*, not from *above*

I had a misconception about where the power of the Holy Spirit came from. When I asked God to pour out His Spirit upon me, I looked for that power to

ome from above. Because of this, I did not recognize
he presence of the Holy Spirit as He began to move.

The power of the Holy Spirit does not come from
above, but from *within*. Jesus said that the Holy Spirit
would come forth from the innermost part of your
being, flowing like rivers of living water.

As a born-again believer, you already have the
power of the Holy Spirit within you just waiting to be
eleased to God in the prayer language of the Spirit.
Releasing the flow of the Spirit within is as natural
and easy as breathing in and out.

All of us, in times of great consecration or inter-
essory prayer, have felt this rising tide of the Holy
Spirit within us. We just did not know it was the
moving of God ready to overflow our lives with the
aptism in the Holy Spirit.

When you feel the Spirit rising up within you, let
t come forth over your vocal cords, and you will
peak in tongues.

ou do the speaking in tongues, not the Holy Spirit

I had so many false ideas about how I would
eceive the Holy Spirit. I really believed that I might
go into a trance-like state and that God would somehow mysteriously communicate through me. I
thought I would just sit still, my mouth would open,
and there would be a voice come from within me that I
ould not control. But the Bible says that on the Day
f Pentecost THEY began to speak with other tongues
s the Spirit gave utterance.

Many times the Spirit tried to take over my
anguage, but I stubbornly refused to stop talking in

English. I wanted the "real thing." I was afraid I would get "in the flesh," and it would be me talking in other tongues, and not the Holy Ghost.

How foolish! Only real, live people in fleshly, human bodies can receive the Holy Spirit. When we leave these bodies, we will not need the baptism in the Holy Spirit. When God baptizes you in the Spirit, it will be *you* talking in other tongues. The Holy Spirit forms the words, but *you* do the speaking.

You cannot speak two languages at the same time. As the power of the Spirit rises within you, stop speaking your known language and, by faith, launch out into "another tongue."

Now you are ready to receive

The psalmist said, *As the hart panteth after the water brooks, so panteth my soul after thee, O God* (Psalm 42:1). Does your soul yearn for God like that? If so, you are ready to receive the baptism in the Holy Spirit.

Find a place to get alone before the Lord. Lift your hands up toward heaven and put your thoughts on the Lord. Focus on the Spirit of God dwelling within you. Put everything else out of your mind.

Now quietly begin to worship and praise the Lord. Rejoice in Him. Say "Praise the Lord," "Glory to God," or "Hallelujah." Whatever you feel in your heart, speak it out loud. Praise the Lord from the depths of your soul.

As you worship the Lord, you will begin to feel the Holy Spirit coming up in your spirit. Now stop speaking in your known language. Let the sighs and yearnings from your innermost being tell God how much you love Him more than you can tell Him in your known language. As the Spirit gives you utterance, just raise your voice to the Lord and let the new words come out.

Speak out whatever small sounds or stammerings come into your mouth. At first, there may be just one or two syllables or words interspersed with the words of your known language. But as you submit to the Spirit, more sounds will come, then words. Repeat whatever sounds come out over and over. As you continue worshiping and magnifying the Lord, the prayer language will begin flowing stronger.

You will not understand the words you are saying because the sounds and the words that come forth are the language of the Spirit speaking directly to God. This language is the scriptural evidence that you have been baptized in the Holy Spirit.

You can speak in tongues every day. This new level of communication with God does not stop with the infilling of the Holy Spirit. It is always available inside you, enabling you to speak to God not only in your language but also in the language created by the Holy Spirit. You will have continuous use of this communication with God that, through it, you may edify your inner man daily and receive new power to be a witness for Jesus Christ.

The baptism in the Holy Spirit is the doorway into the nine gifts of the Spirit found in 1 Corinthians 12:1-11 and the supernatural power of God. This blessed experience will revolutionize your life for God!

BOOKS BY JOHN OSTEEN

*A Miracle For Your Marriage
*A Place Called There
*ABC's of Faith
*Believing God For Your Loved Ones
 Deception! Recognizing True and False Ministries
 Four Principles in Receiving From God
*Healed of Cancer by Dodie Osteen
*How To Claim the Benefits of the Will
*How To Demonstrate Satan's Defeat
 How To Flow in the Super Supernatural
 How To Minister Healing to the Sick
*How To Receive Life Eternal
 How To Release the Power of God
 Keep What God Gives
*Love & Marriage
 Overcoming Hindrances To Receiving the Baptism in the Holy Spirit
*Overcoming Opposition: How To Succeed in Doing the Will of God
     by Lisa Comes
*Pulling Down Strongholds
*Receive the Holy Spirit
 Reigning in Life as a King
 Rivers of Living Water
 Saturday's Coming
 Seven Facts About Prevailing Prayer
 Seven Qualities of a Man of Faith
*Six Lies the Devil Uses To Destroy Marriages by Lisa Comes
 Spiritual Food For Victorious Living
*The Believer's #1 Need
 The Bible Way to Spiritual Power
 The Confessions of a Baptist Preacher
*The Divine Flow
*The 6th Sense...Faith
 The Truth Shall Set You Free
*There Is a Miracle in Your Mouth
 This Awakening Generation
 Unraveling the Mystery of the Blood Covenant
*What To Do When Nothing Seems To Work
*What To Do When the Tempter Comes
 You Can Change Your Destiny

*Also available in Spanish.

Please write for a complete list of prices in the John Osteen Library.
Lakewood Church • P.O. Box 23297 • Houston, Texas 77228